What Did Jesus Promise?

By Helen Haidle

Illustrated by Cheri Bladholm

What Did Jesus Promise?
Copyright © 1999 by Helen Haidle
Illustrations © 1999 by Cheri Bladholm

Requests for information should be addressed to:

Zonder**kidz**

The Children's Group of ZondervanPublishingHouse
Grand Rapids, Michigan 49530
www.zonderkidz.com

Zonderkidz is a trademark of The Zondervan Corporation
What Did Jesus Promise? was previously published by Gold 'n' Honey formerly a division of Multnomah Publishers, Inc.

Library of Congress Cataloging-in-Publication Data:
Haidle, Helen.
    What did Jesus Promise? / by Helen Haidle.
        p. cm.
        Summary: Presents sixteen selections from the Bible containing promises which Jesus spoke concerning forgiveness, prayer, giving, and heaven.
        ISBN: 1-57673-649-0
        1. Jesus Christ–Promises Juvenile literature. [1. Jesus Christ–Promises. 2. Bible. N.T.–Selections.] I. Title.
BT 306.H24 1999
232–dc21
        99-22616
        CIP

Scripture quotations are from: *The Holy Bible*, New King James Version (NKJV) Copyright © 1984 by Thomas Nelson, Inc. Also quoted: *The Holy Bible*, New International Version (NIV) © 1973, 1984 by International Bible Society, used by permission of Zondervan Publishing House; *The Living Bible* (TLB) © 1971, used by permission of Tyndale House Publishers, Inc. All rights reserved.

All rights reserved. No part of this publication may be reproduced, stored in a retrieval system, or transmitted, in any form or by any means—electronic, mechanical, photocopying, recording, or any other—without prior permission of the publisher.

Design by Open Door Design
Printed in China

99 00 01 02 03 04 / HK / 10 9 8 7 6 5 4 3 2 1

> **"**For God so loved the world that He gave His only begotten Son, that whosoever believes in Him should have eternal life. **"**
>
> **John 3:16**

Who is Jesus?

Jesus is the Son of God.

He died on a cross for your sins.

And then He came alive again!

Jesus loves you.

You can trust Him to keep His promises.

"Blessed are those

who have not

seen [Me] and

yet have believed."

John 20:29

Jesus promised to bless you if you believe in Him.
It's not always easy to believe in something—
or Someone—you can't see.

"Do not worry

about your life,

what you will eat...

Consider the ravens...

God feeds them...

But seek the

kingdom of God,

and all these

things shall be

added to you."

Luke 12:22, 24, 31

Jesus promised to take care of you.
Make Jesus the most
important part of your life.
Then you won't have to
worry about anything.

"Blessed are

the peacemakers,

for they shall

be called

sons of God."

Matthew 5:9

Jesus promised
to bless you when
you make peace.
Get along with
other people and
help them get along
with each other.

"If you remain in

me and my words

remain in you,

ask whatever you

wish, and it will

be given you."

John 15:7 (NIV)

Jesus promised to answer your prayers.
Get to know Him well. Then you will
know how He wants you to pray.

⁶⁶Peace I leave with

you, My peace

I give to you...

Let not your heart

be troubled, neither

let it be afraid.⁹⁹

John 14:27

Jesus promised to
give you His peace.
He will help to calm you
when you feel afraid or upset.

"For if you forgive [others] when they sin against you, your heavenly Father will also forgive you."

Matthew 6:14 (NIV)

Jesus promised that God will forgive you if you forgive others. Jesus will help you to forgive.

⁶⁶I have set you an example that you should do as I have done for you.... Now that you know these things, you will be blessed if you do them.⁹⁹

John 13:15, 17 (NIV)

Jesus promised to bless you
when you serve others as He did.
Always be helpful and kind.

"For if you give, you

will get! Your gift

will return to

you in full and

overflowing measure...

whatever measure

you use to give—

large or small—

will be used to

measure what is

given back to you."

Luke 6:38 (TLB)

Jesus promised that everyone
who gives to others will receive.
Be generous when you give.

"Take care! Don't do your good deeds publicly, to be admired...but when you do a kindness to someone, do it secretly...and your Father who knows all secrets will reward you."

Matthew 6:1-4 (TLB)

Jesus promised to reward you
when you are kind to others.
But do your good deeds secretly
and don't brag about them.

"If anyone gives

even a cup of cold

water to one of

these little ones...

he will certainly

not lose his reward."

Matthew 10:42 (NIV)

Jesus promised to reward even

the smallest things you do.

He sees them all, even when others don't.

"When you put on a dinner...invite the poor, the crippled, the lame, and the blind. Then at the resurrection of the godly, God will reward you for inviting those who can't repay you."

Luke 14:12-14 (TLB)

Jesus promised to bless you when you help people who cannot repay you. Someday He will repay you.

"Blessed are you when people insult you, persecute you and falsely say all kinds of evil against you because of me. Rejoice and be glad, because great is your reward in heaven."

Matthew 5:11-12 (NIV)

Jesus promised to reward those who follow Him. Live for Jesus, even when others make fun of you.

"In My Father's house

are many mansions....

I go to prepare

a place for you...

I will come again

and receive you to

Myself; that where

I am, there you

may be also."

John 14:2-3

Jesus promised to make
a home for you in Heaven.
You will live with Him forever.

"They will see the Son

of Man coming on

the clouds of heaven

with power and

great glory. And He

will send His angels

with a great sound

of a trumpet,

and they will gather

together His elect

from...one end of

heaven to the other."

Matthew 24:30-31

Jesus promised to come back to earth.
He came first as a helpless baby.
He will come back as the King of kings.

66 Be sure of this—

that I am with you

always, even to the

end of the world. 99

M a t t h e w   2 8 : 2 0

Jesus promised to
be with you always.
He loves you.
And He will never
leave you.